PUNCHING OUT

JIM DANIELS

PUNCHING OUT

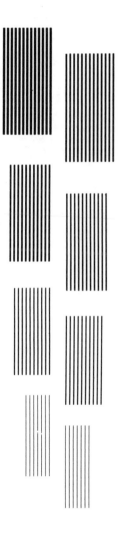

WAYNE STATE UNIVERSITY PRESS DETROIT

Copyright ©1990 by Wayne State University Press,
Detroit Michigan 48201. All rights are
reserved.
No part of this book may be reproduced
without formal permission
Manufactured in the United States.

99 98 97   7 6 5 4

Library of Congress Cataloging-in-Publication Data

Daniels, Jim.
    Punching out / Jim Daniels.
        p.   cm.
    ISBN 0-8143-2190-9.—ISBN 0-8143-2191-7 (pbk.)
    1. Automobile industry workers—Poetry.   2. Automobile factories—Poetry.
    3. Working class—Poetry.   4. Work—Poetry.   I. Title.
    PS3554.A5635P86   1990
    811'.54—dc20   89-16662
                                                                        CIP

The greatest defeat, in anything, is to forget, and above all to forget what it is that has smashed you, and to let yourself be smashed without ever realizing how thoroughly devilish men can be. When our time is up, we musn't bear malice, but neither must we forget: we must tell the whole thing, without altering one word,—everything that we have seen of man's viciousness; and then it will be over and time to go. That is enough of a job for a whole lifetime.

Céline

CONTENTS

ACKNOWLEDGMENTS

These poems appeared in the following magazines, often in slightly different form:

Blue Light Review: "Signing"
Bombay Gin: "Heaven Enough," "Timers," "Photo Opportunity"
Corridors: "Big Shit"
Cutbank: "Bush's Story"
Flipside: "Pieces"
Iowa Review: "Midnight Ramble," "You Bet," "Elephant House," "Work Song: Bucket"
Laurel Review: "Paul P. Was Here"
New England Review/Bread Loaf Quarterly: "Sweeping Stoned"
Paris Review: "Going Up and Down"
Pig Iron: "Quality/Control," "Called Back," "The Costs"
Quarry: "Santino"
Quarterly West: "Midnight Date," "Not Working"
Quindaro: "Factory Education"
West Branch: "Hard Rock"
Wooster Review: "Intro to Foreman Psych"
Wormwood Review: "Cowboy Gets Fired," "Plant Nurse's Story," "Odie's Story," "Back to the Basics," "Midnight Ramble," "Exits," "But"

Some of these poems also appeared in two chapbooks, *Factory Poems*, Jack-in-the-Box Press, and *On the Line*, Signpost Press, and in *Going for Coffee*, Harbour Publishing, an anthology of poems about work.

Special thanks to Gerald Costanzo, David James, Kristin Kovacic, Frank Lehner, Mike Rose, Timothy Russell, Lee Ann Schreiner, and Bruce Severy for their help with this book.

1 BASIC TRAINING

Hear
This?
WEAR EAR
PROTECTION

YOUR safety is OUR business

EYES
ONLY TWO TO A CUSTOMER
PROTECT THEM!

PROTECT YOUR HANDS
WEAR GLOVES
Keep hands clear
WATCH
for sharp objects

Daydreams Can Cause NIGHTMARES

IN THE MIDNIGHT ZONE

This your first day? Bush asks.
I been here 22 fuckin' years.
I was gonna work here two years. He pauses.
The whiskey hangs in my face.
Twenty-two FUCKING years, he shouts
above the machines' pound and hiss.
No one looks. He throws a tube in the aisle
to make his point.

Foreman Santino runs up yelling
Settle your ass down—
the kid's gonna think
he's supposed to act like a maniac too.
    It's gotten me this far. Bush spits
out his cigar, picks up the tube.

Grab a few of these things.
Bush lifts four tubes off hooks,
throws them on the floor—soft belly
strong arms, tattooed and burned.
Take one, put it in the welder.
He slams one between two clamps.
Slip in a clip. Press the idiot buttons.
He grunts. *Grab another tube.*
The machine spits, welding
the tiny brake-line clip onto the tube.
Get the idea, kid?
He glares at me, belching whiskey:
Now you do one.

See that fucker over there with the hat
he points to a slick black dude
fedora cocked over one eye.
He's the laziest motherfucker
you'll ever see. Don't ever
do anything for that fucker,
Bush shouts, but the dude ignores him.
Bush tosses another tube
and it sparks off the cement floor.

*Hey lazy-ass fucker, when you gonna do
some work?* The dude jumps out of the way.
Fastest he's moved in years, Bush says.
The dude pulls a switchblade, waves it
in the air, points it at Bush
and smiles.

Ah, go fuck yourself
Bush yells across the aisle.

Dude grabs me at break, smiles:
Name's Spooner. He's stoned to the bone,
his head lolling from side to side.
*That dude's crazy, man.
Tomorrow, you work on my side.
Show you how this job's
really done.*

WHERE I'M AT: FACTORY EDUCATION

My first week, I'm working the cover welder
when the automatic welding gun stops
being automatic halfway through a cover.

I rush down the aisle to find Santino,
biting my lip, sweat in my eyes.
The other guys stop working to watch.
Santino gets Old Green, the jobsetter,
to fix my machine.

Later, Spooner grabs me by the neck
pushes my head against the machine.
Old Green shouts into my face:
You ain't supposed to go get Santino,
he's got to find you, dig?
what's the big hurry, boy? Listen,
You get paid the same no matter.
Kissing ass good way
to get your lips burned.
He walks away. Spooner lets go,
stands there a minute, shakes his head:
Where you at, brother, where you at?

∎

Santino shows me a new job:
After the machine cuts the tubes
hang them on these hooks.

I pick them up, hang them,
pick, hang, till the edges slice
moons into my hands. I stop.
The line backs up.

Santino slaps my bloody hands,
grabs my shirt: *Where's*
your goddamn gloves?

The plant nurse tapes my hands.
When I get back, Santino throws me

leather gloves: *Next time
you're fired.*

I shove anger deep
into rough leather. I forget
and work fast.

Where you at, brother?

■

Bush idles over from his broken machine
big pot sticking out tight
under a white t-shirt
grey hair slicked back, perfect.
He bends toward me and stares
at my greasy coveralls. I sweat
behind the washer, tossing
axle parts into baskets.

*Hey, look at me.
Am I dirty? Am I sweating?
Look, you got to learn how to survive
around here, kid. If you don't know
how to break your machine
then you shouldn't be runnin' it.*
He wanders off, shaking his head.

I push my safety glasses up my nose.
The parts start backing up
so I toss them sloppy in the baskets,
pause to straighten the rows,
get farther behind.

A part glides crooked down the conveyor
and I rush to straighten it
but catch myself. It catches
on the washer's inside edge.

Parts pile up behind the jammed piece.
The conveyor chain clicks, then snaps.
I press the *Stop* button.

Bush walks by and smiles,
patting his belly.
Sit your ass down, kid.
When Santino comes
look stupid. Like this.

∎

Santino rushes over. His shirt says
"Your Safety is *Our* Business."
You bet I work safely—I just point
to the machine, and thumbs down.
He can't touch it—it's not his job.
See if you can fix it, he says.
Not my job, I say.
He calls Old Green
who looks at it and says
Not my job—
need an electrician.
The electrician shows up
but he just wants to jive
with Nita, the fox
who works at the next press.
Santino gets on his case
which *is* his job
and the electrician
fixes the machine
which is *his* job
and I go back to my idiot buttons.
Which is *my* job.
I work safely.

Where you at?

SANTINO

Pale blob of cold light.
He never sweats. The Man of No Smiles.
He must wear ice packs under his shirt.

Behind his back all the boys ape his walk
and his always pointing finger
that says *Come with me.*
When Santino points at you
you best turn to steel to block his rage.
He puts you places you don't want to go.

Santino only sees numbers.
He sneaks bad parts past Quality Control
for his numbers. But his numbers
are low. We see to that.

Santino comes, you stand up and work
or pretend or hide or go
the other way.

He made one dude run the broacher
when it was squirting oil
and that man lost a hand.
Santino made him a sweeper.

FACTORY COOL

Spooner wears tinted sunglasses
with his initials
in rhinestones on the side
and a felt hat with a big brim.
He smokes thin cigars.
Coveralls unbuttoned to his navel.
Gold chains. Clean welding gloves
in his back pocket, just for show.
He painted footprints on the floor,
memorized the steps that keep him clean.
Dyed his safety shoes white.

One day I worked his machine—
tried to stay in his footprints
got twisted up and fell.
No one noticed. I pulled myself up—
what's his payoff?—blew my nose
into a greasy sleeve.

SHIFT CHANGE

I bump into my pal, Odie
standing by the guardhouse
drinking a beer, trying to get
suspended. He needs time off
to study for night-school exams.
He's studying criminal justice
to get a job that pays
half what he makes here.

Hey Digger, want a beer,
he yells at me. *No,*
but I see you've got one.
The guard's headed this way.
He tosses the beer—a high arc
anyone could see.

I walk away while he pleads
with the guard, laying it on.
If they think he's trying
to get caught they might think
he's crazy. Then he'd be in
real trouble.

GLOVE/HAND

The hands have trouble being naked.
The hand has trouble with the pen.

In the gloves the fingers do not feel
hot or cold or sharp.
The gloves make the hands
part of a machine.

The gloved hand is a paw,
an awkward, swiping thing.

Without claws.
The glove gets the job done.
The hand has little to say.

GRAFFITI

Rock 'n roll
Coors and cunt

KY's house is being cased
KY sucks

Paul P. was hear also

Nigger/Negro/Black
What color are assholes?

Klan country.
Bullshit!

Fatboy Santino

War on fags

Fuck is a better idea

Bruno's Bar   No grill

my safety is none of your bizness

Get in shape at Ford Tanny

No Mo Fo Mo Co

Wally was framed

walkout
walkout at 3

Have you ever recieved head
while wisiling dixie?

Be artistic
Fuck you

MUSCLES

The transfer that carries
housings from welder to water tester
gets busted bad, run into by a hi-lo.

Santino shouts, *You, Digger,*
carry the fuckin' housings over.

Truck housings, the heaviest. I stare,
wanting to spark his eyes out
with a welding torch. I shuffle
to the growing pile on the floor.
Santino stares, hands on hips
motions for me to speed up.

I hug the metal logs
lug them across to Odie
working the water tester
who helps when he can.

Old Green, working on the transfer,
laughs, *Fuck Santino.*
He puts his hand on my shoulder.
Take it easy, man. This job'll
put muscles in your shit.

I pretend to be strong
slow down my work song
to allow for the new weight.
I drop a couple on the floor
just to hear the sound.
During break I drink water till it hurts.

At quitting time Old Green yells,
points to his ass. Nodding his head,
he mouths the word *Muscles.*

At home I sit on the can
my shit weak and runny
the knots untied.

EXITS

After parking my car in the East Lot, I head past the guard post, past the security cameras, past the sign listing the number of days since the last work-loss accident, stuck at *29* for weeks. Then into the locker room, with its large round sinks, and the hand cleaner that looks and feels like sawdust, and the old battered lockers, and the first whiff of the dark smell of grease.

The plant has its own hospital, its own store, its own railroad, its own streets, a main cafeteria and five satellites. I got lost the first few times just trying to find my way out at shift change. Once I ended up at the wrong doors, the ones that go from noise and grit and darkness to clean, bright, quiet offices where people dress nice and talk to each other in normal voices. Heads turned. I turned, back into the black noise. Lost.

WORK SONG: BUCKET

Ain't got no food
in my lunch bucket
in my lunch bucket
just a fruit pie
a sugar-bomb red-chunk
hard-crust goo-face fruit pie
I can lick it or suck it
or chuck it
like it was muck or a hockey puck
ain't got no luck
in my lunch bucket
but I won't cry
I'll just say fuck it
fuckit. bucket.

EXCHANGE

When Santino hands me my check today
he puts his hand on my shoulder
like it means something. And it feels enough
like it really does mean something
for me to smile at him
like it means something.

2 | FACTORY STUD

To All Employees:

The Plant Management sincerely regrets that the Open House scheduled for Saturday and Sunday, June 10 and 11, has to be postponed.

The large number of employees working, industrial vehicle activity in the plant, and associated machinery in operation scheduled last weekend, raised a question of the safety of family members and visitors touring the plant under those operating conditions.

I again apologize for the postponement. While many employees expressed their disappointment, most agreed that the heavy weekend schedule made it impractical to have our families tour the plant at that time.

Plant Manager

FACTORY STUD

A guy at orientation told me
*Listen dude, whatever happens
don't end up in department 53 or 16.
They'll bust your ass
hauling truck axles.*

I ended up in 53, heaving
the heavy housings onto pallets.
Started out sore and shaking
but after a month or so
I got muscles.

And when a new-hire asks me
What department?
I say, *53,*
in a matter-of-fact casual tone,
tight smile, little squint.

PAUL PAKOWSKI WAS HERE

After 38 years, his job
simplified itself
to two phrases:
Fuck foreman.
Go slow.

He shuffles his bent back
sits when he can
on an empty welding-coil barrel.
Came from Poland 40 years ago
still doesn't know English.
Waiting for retirement
he scratches his name
onto machines and walls:
Paul P was hear

I work the machine next to him.
He passes the parts over
and motions to me with his hands
like a calmly drowning man
trying to push the water down.
Fuck foreman. I nod,
shout above the metal sounds:
Go slow.

BUTCH, THE UNION MAN

Butch, our committeeman,
wears a bowling shirt
that says *"Butch" Leshinski.*
And *Committeeman*
where it usually says *Captain.*

Butch says *Call me Butch.*
He smells like Aqua Velva and cheap cigars.
He is supposed to help me.
What's the beef? he says.

I'm a young punk.
Butch puts his arm around Santino.
You ain't got no beef, he says.

REPLACING DAVE THE SWEEPER

I caught on fast
how to take half an hour
looking for soap for the mop bucket,
wheeling it around in circles,
waving at the guys on the line.

How to lean on the broom
and watch for Santino
while hidden between
huge rolls of steel
back against the wall.
How to move slow
but never stop moving,
to count off the seconds
for each step
each push of the broom,
to be clumsy and stupid,
staring at the ground
like an old lover
just going through the motions.

SWEEPING STONED

I slide across the floor
doing my factory Fred Astaire
on grease I should be mopping up.

I put my shovel through
the parts washer. Nothing
like a clean shovel. Do it
a couple more times.

I wave to the overhead crane man,
the only one who can see me
hidden between rolls of steel.
I mimic his hand signals.
He makes the *crazy* sign.

I turn on the steam gun
and spray down the dies
pulled from presses for cleaning.
Lost in a cloud of steam,
I'm Sherlock Holmes
taking a break
from the investigation.

I sweep in the smallest circles
singing to myself the littlest song:
what a nice broom
what a nice job
what a nice ringing in my ears.

HEAT DOCTOR

In the plant cafeteria
Spooner rips off the cold-drink machine—
reaches up from the bottom with his long arms,
yanks the cartons down.
He squishes some, and we throw them out.

He passes out the good ones.
We line up around him like expectant parents:
Will it be a lemonade—
lemonade or iced tea?

BACK TO THE BASICS

I draw pictures of naked women
on the axle covers I weld
and send them down the line
to the other guys.
This helps keep my memory intact.
They think I am a real artist.

This inside-seam weld
looks like a grey vagina to me.
I stare at every woman I see,
each imagined breast and buttock.

I find a *Newsweek* during break.
Dave says *That ain't no
pussy book you lookin' at ya know.*
I throw it down—who wants to read
about politics anyway.
He says *I got pussy books.*
I follow him.

WORK SONG: FACTORY MUSICAL

The whole line broke down
so we was all standing round
when Spooner picked
up two welding sticks
and started banging away
on an axle housing
playing that factory beat—
all of us gathered around,
it was a Friday.

Clapping hands
and old Paul P.
plump and slow in coveralls
tapping one foot
and then the other
shaking and dancing
round and round
and singing a song
in another tongue.

Nita started a disco dance
and Odie dancing hoedown style
and we was hopping and bopping
all down aisle C
when Santino came
but laughed and shrugged
and clapped in time
with the factory beat
just drums no horns no strings just
boompa tappa boompa tappa

then our man Spooner
moved around
tappa tappa on the floor
boompa boompa on machine
and on the welding helmet of old Paul P.
like Hollywood
and we all dancing shouting

Go go goooo!
and even old Jess
ready to retire
managed to smile his dance

we all so proud and flaunting sweating
the music pounding inside
until all the sudden
it was time
to return to the line.

HEAVEN ENOUGH

Odie and I punch in and find
the day shift's left us
six good stacks of blanks
lined up in front of the press.

Cold outside—sleet, slush.
The coffee between our hands first break
is heaven enough to take our time over.

At lunch, I splurge on Twinkies,
shove them in my face.
Digger, my man, you are a twinkie,
Odie says. I talk with my mouth full.

Last break, Nita shakes her butt and sings
Aretha: *Chain, chain, chain . . .
chain of fools.* We whistle and clap.
*That's what you all be,
a chain of fools,* she laughs. We nod.

Even on the job, I'm happy, happy
for no reason, stacking the blanks
like I'm building something
I could hold onto. The press crunches
down, bends the metal.
I just nod and sing.

PUTTING IT IN NEUTRAL

Working in a factory is like taking off
in a plane, I tell Odie, *then*
you go into neutral and just hang there.
At quitting time you land
right where you started.
Maybe you never land, or land
forty years down the road and crash.

A few beers at Bruno's
and I start figuring it all out.
Odie just laughs and flies his hands
over the bar, making airplane noises.

I never used to get into fights
till I took this job, I tell him.
What's that supposed to mean? Odie asks.

I don't know. I twist the stool around.
I used to meet more women too.
I used to be a pretty suave guy.

He laughs:
Mr. Suave, eh?
From Mr. Suave to Mr. Neutral.
He shakes his head, waves his hand at me,
What a comedian.

Back home, drying off from my shower,
I spit on the bathroom floor.
I clean it up—what gear's this?

LITTLE FACTORY

Today I bought myself a boom box out of some guy's trunk in the parking lot. *Quality merchandise,* he said. It doesn't work right. I should know all about *quality* by now.

The radio blares disco hits. I'm stuck with AM but I try to shake my ass a little on the seat, to lose myself in sound. Bumps in the road help the bounce. I'm so pumped up I could almost squeeze this steering wheel into dust. I speed up and two cats in the road scramble away.

I go to the Quik Pik. A cop stops me for not having my lights on. I show him baseball cards and ice cream. He asks if I've been drinking. *Not yet* I say. My little sister's making out with her boyfriend on the corner. I honk my horn at them, flash my brights. *Asshole,* my sister shouts. I don't hear nothing from her boyfriend.

Sleep. I need it. Up all night, lying on my bed in the basement, I crack another beer and tell the dog that everything's fucked up. He eats a bug. Today I took a pair of greasy gloves home by accident. There they sit in the corner of my room, my own little factory. I fall asleep and dream: I am killing cats.

REVELATIONS

Music is noise. Noise is music.

If you don't say *fuck* no one takes you seriously.

There are a fucking million ways to push two buttons.

Being all out of steel is the opposite of being all out of dope.

FUN ON THE LINE

Gracie wants a kiss,
Junior says. *Who wants*
to kiss Gracie?
Hey Cowboy, come over here
and give Gracie a kiss.

Fat Gracie squats in her t-shirt
with *outrageous* written across the breasts.
She quietly rams brakes onto axles.

Hey Gracie, show us the tattoo on your leg!
Yeah, c'mon Gracie, we wanna see your fuckin' tattoo.

The axles roll down the line.
Gracie flips us the bird
grabs another brake
never gets behind.

SMALL CATCH

He cut the power
but the cutters were still going.

The ambulance races up
they toss the bleeding finger in
with the man and race off.
Everyone looks for a second
then goes back to work:
a finger.

TIMERS

A man with a stopwatch stares
at my hands, his thumb on the button.
He is timing how long it takes me
to take this part, put it in my machine,
push two buttons, take it out.

He is trying to eliminate my job.
But I take a second or two
to scratch my balls.
Got to allow time for that,
I wink at him.

He shakes his head,
his bright orange earplugs
wedged in tight.

I guess finally it's not him
who decides. He seems reluctant
to meet my eyes, jotting quick notes
in the aisle.

Somebody somewhere's got a watch
on him too. Somebody's put us both here
where we can't hear each other.

COWBOY GETS FIRED

We call them cookie-cutters—
huge presses punching out steel cookies.
You stand on a platform
and feed blank discs into two presses,
running back and forth
to keep them both loaded.
Used to be a two-man job.

I worked that job one day in summer heat.
Running back and forth, sweat soaking
my coveralls, shoes, I started hating myself
up on that platform. But I needed the money
so I kept feeding, feeding
till I slipped and fell.
Old Green stopped the presses.
I ran to the bathroom and soaked
my body in water. Driving home,
I swore I'd quit
before I did that job again.

Next day when Cowboy walked off the platform
and got fired, the union didn't do
anything—he didn't have his 90 days in.
I wanted to quit in support
but I wiped my hands
and took his place.

MIDNIGHT DATE
for Alice

After calling you on my last break
I watch the sun set over rolls of steel
rusting in the factory yard.

Old Green lies on some greasy cardboard,
hands folded over his chest.
He opens his eyes, looks at me
closes them again.

I close my eyes and see your shiny hair
fall across my face. Santino calls
me back, shoots me with a finger.

∎

I put on earphones, safety glasses,
shove my hands into sweaty leather
and stand in dim light waiting
for axle housings to rattle down
the line, drop their grey weight
into my hands. I throw my head back
and howl your name: two more hours.

∎

Santino gives the *break* sign.
I toss my gloves in a barrel,
punch my card, wash up.

I leave the locker room
with clean hands and step out
into what I want to believe
is a skyful of good will,
is a parking lot lined with possibility.

Tonight the moon looks full enough
to feed a lot of hearts. Mine rises
like the bird furthest from this factory.

Tonight let's shed our clothes
and dance in this cool air.
Let's taste the moon's
clean white meat.

3 | THE VILLAGE IDIOT

Ronald Ebens and his stepson Michael Nitz, both former auto workers, beat Vincent Chin to death with a baseball bat outside a Detroit nightclub. They apparently thought Chin was Japanese and blamed him for the industry's joblessness. Both received probation for manslaughter.

NOT WORKING

The city lights on the hill
across the river from this concrete
park are not winking at me.
They are singing a song
about briefcases and broken pianos.

This night, a black limousine
speeds past, drops a bundle
of ticking stars in front of me.
Messed up on cheap wine, in the middle
of all this business, I cough up a hawker
spit it into the river.

The hand on my shoulder could be
the soft weight of the night, could be
an unfolding angry fist. It is
the hand of *No Friend,* of *Move On.*

Someone is always calling me
away at such moments of clear vision
with words like *property* and *law.*

In the morning, I will join the line
curling around the corner like a smashed
snake, twitching a bit at the end. Yes,
I will wait my turn like the rest of them,
my fists unclenching like alarm clocks.

I sit on the stoop of my father's house,
allowing myself this luxury, untaxed
and uninvited. I tug on my beard,
hum and rock like the village idiot.
I sit for a long time. I hum so quietly
not even the mailbox hears me.

IN LINE

I stand in line with the rest of them
shuffle my feet on the floor,
shifting my weight from foot to foot
like a naked kid in line
for a football physical.
Nowhere to hide. Eyes on the floor.

I have no skills. That's what
I'll learn here today.

COSTS

I press my nose to the screen
and wait for the dog.
Dark sky tonight—the moon
getting some time off too.

I think of the numbers.
How many cars America buys
determines whether I work
or not, whether I have money
or not. My dog jangles
as he trots around the corner
and the music of his chain hits
a warm spot. I crouch next to him.
Our breath steams the air.
He licks my face, glad to have me home.

Maybe I buy his friendship
with food. He is trained
to accept the chain, to wait patiently
while I hook and unhook it.

I do not miss the noise and sweat.
I may get called back soon,
or I may not. I let the dog
back into the house.
They have lists.
My bank account dwindles.
I hang the chain on its hook.
I search for more ways to save.

CALLED BACK

Driving down the same bumpy road
I fight to get my place back.

I know the way—which lot to park in
which lane to turn down.
I whoosh a fly out the window
slamming into Park:
the same grey coveralls,
same broken glass.

Past the guard, punch the card,
new production number, new gloves—
same old grease and dim lights.

For lunch I eat the same meat,
the same stale bread.
Friends are still friends
and assholes, assholes.

The quarters I drop
into the coffee machine
sing a song I have memorized
despite my lack of faith.
I fold my hands around the cup
thinking about how much I need
this job: the first bitter sip.

4 | HARD ROCK

MANUAL ON GENERAL SAFE PRACTICES

Your plans for tomorrow depend on safety to-
day.

Do not enter a roped off area without authori-
zation of the supervisory employee who is re-
sponsible for roping it off.

Foreign bodies may be removed from eyes only
by medical personnel.

Drink water only from such approved sources
as regular drinking fountains.

Move gassed people only to fresh air and then
call medical help.

Do not use defective tools. Use the right
tools.

Avoid any form of horseplay or fighting.

Walk—do not run.

NO GLOVES

No new gloves today—
a mix-up in that mysterious area
we never see, the offices up front.

We poke into a basket of used gloves
like it's a basket of body parts,
afraid to touch anything.

I stick my hands
into two clammy gloves
discarded by the day shift.
I stick my hands
into two dead tongues
and stick out my own
as dead as the others.

SIGNING

lunch: open your mouth. Put your hand in front of it. Rapidly open and close the hand.

need paint: slap paint across your face with a big brush.

need hi-lo: steer a steering wheel.

break: snap an arm in two.

need banjo housings: strum one.

need housing covers: draw a circle around your head.

need cigarette or joint: fingers to lips.

need drink: thumb in air, fingers in fist, raised to lips.

need welding sticks: play drums.

need overhead crane: point to rafters, twirl finger.

faster: finger twirling in circle.

slower: hands pushing down.

no: you know that one.

no way: point to crotch.

foreman coming: tighten a tie.

machine broke down: point to machine, thumbs down.

disgust: wave hand down and away.

fuck you: you know that one.

HARD ROCK

*You see, when you're a kid in a factory town, you got only
two choices—staying and enduring the factory life, or
getting out. But either way, you gotta be tough, you have
to refuse to give up. People in Detroit are faced with more
pressure than kids in other cities. There's got to be a
release for the frustrations, and Detroiters express that
release through rock 'n roll.*

—Peter Wolf

A bunch of guys walk out
because it's over a hundred
and the bosses are passing out
pink salt tablets and saying
Get to work, like it's a normal day.

We stand around the parking lot
drinking beers. Spooner opens up his van
and puts his speakers on the roof,
booms out some kick-ass tunes. One by one
the guys take off their shirts
put down their beers and start boogying.

Somebody might say *Look at these guys—
if they can dance, they can work.*
The plant manager standing by the gate
with a couple security guards
might be saying that right now.
He's the kind of guy who doesn't appreciate
good music. The kind of guy who'd say
This is not a pretty sight.
The sweat shines off beer guts,
dribbles down over tattoos, scars, medals,
flies through the air, everyone slick,
stomping their boots on the ground,
smelling tar, oil, and their own bodies,
their own bodies sweating because they want to,
and the crowd keeps getting bigger,
and we keep shouting
Louder, louder.

WORK BOOTS: STILL LIFE

Next to the screen door
work boots dry in the sun.
Salt lines map the leather
and the laces droop
like the arms of a new-hire
waiting to punch out.
The shoe hangs open like the sigh
of someone too tired to speak
a mouth that can almost breathe.
A tear in the leather reveals
a shiny steel toe
a glimpse of the hard promise of safety
the promise of steel and the years to come.

QUALITY/CONTROL

Uncle Jim wanders over
blowing smoke from a big cigar.
I'm a healthy Clint Eastwood—
I smoke fat cigars. He retires
in three weeks. He winks, drunk again
on his *Eye-talian lunch.*

Lemme look at them parts.
I pull a banjo housing from a basket.
They're all cracking, I tell him.
I think the steel's bad.
He rubs his gloved hand
over the crack in the rim, caresses it.
Nah, nothing wrong with this steel.
I ain't never seen a bad piece of steel
and I ain't never seen
a bad piece of ass.

■

He dances down Aisle M
with balloons on his head.
He tells all the young women
Call me Uncle Jim

He wears a jockstrap outside his pants
apples and oranges falling out.
He sits down, out of breath,
puffs on his smoke.
I find a quiet place for him to sleep.
The parts roll by,
the parts roll by.

ODIE'S STORY

Uncle Jim thinks he's a connoisseur of cigars, so my sister, who works in the R.G. Dunn factory, gets these cases for dollar cigars and puts 25-cent cigars in them and I take them to work and give them to the dude and he's smelling them and going around saying *Now you want to smell a good cigar, smell this.* And everybody else knows except him that they're only cheap cigars. You know, he seemed so fucking happy I finally couldn't tell him. As much as I don't like the guy, he seemed real grateful. It made his day. I mean I've never seen anybody get so excited over cigars.

4TH OF JULY IN THE FACTORY

No trouble finding a parking spot today.
No line at the time clocks.
I walk past the deserted, motionless
assembly line in department 65,
past the dark cafeteria.

A doubleheader at Tiger Stadium.
Somebody shouts the first-game score.
I can actually hear him, his voice echoing.

Santino smiles at the thought
of all the money he will make today.
I smile with him.

When the big press breaks down
Jess, press repairman, motions
thumbs down and walks away.
We sit and tell jokes
waiting for Santino
to come by and notice.

Bush brought in a bottle
and we pass it around.
Even K.Y., the hi-lo driver
gets off his seat and takes a hit.

When Santino shows up
he threatens to send us home
but instead sends us on early lunch
while an electrician works on the press.

We go outside to sit
on huge rolls of steel
and watch the sun set.
How wonderful it is
to make triple time
for sitting on our asses,
how wonderful to hear our own voices
even our own hearts beating.

IT AIN'T MUCH BUT IT'S A

Big firecracker fight 4th of July
broke a few windows. Earned our triple-time.
While the cat's away

That woman working the next press wears tight clothes.
Holes in her ass to prove it.
If you've got it

At lunch the men brag about themselves—
sex machines that never break down.
Put your money where

A squirt gun fight ends in a real fight
and a real gun.
Boys will be

A hi-lo driver can't stop
and smashes a foreman into the wall.
Accidents will

PROPOSAL

3:30 a.m. Insomnia's taken hold.
Reading yesterday's paper I see a picture
of Caroline Kennedy going back to work
after lunch on the 4th of July.

So, even some of the famous
have to work on the holiday too.
I imagine my picture there and laugh.

Caroline, did a security guard check
your lunch for booze? Did you get stoned
because the bosses weren't around?

I did. It was hot in the factory—
they gave us free pop and salt pills.
How was your air-conditioned office?

Maybe I have no right to criticize
having grown up here so far from the limelight.

We're about the same age.
I've never had my picture in the paper.
Would you marry me?

BIG SHIT

At break time
we shuffle into the satellite cafeteria
push the mop man aside
ignore his yelling
track grease over the wet floor.
We come to stand face to face
with the shit rack—
the candy machine, cupcake machine, gum machine
chips machine, hot foods machine, cold foods machine
coffee machine, juice machine, pop machine
milk machine, change machine.
We shove our quarters in, slam buttons
grab plastic.

∎

When the machine man comes
whoever needs money tells him
they lost some change.
Pale and thin in his clean clothes
he wrinkles his nose up because we stink,
dishes out change to men
he knows are lying.
He's learned not to argue.
We make him sweat
the bad kind of sweat
and take him for his quarters.

∎

When it's time to head back
the mop man comes in to clean up our mess.
We stop at the john
and whoever has to shit, shits—
we got a club—biggest turd wins the pot.

We don't let Bush in on it anymore.
That fat man won two weeks straight.
We put his biggest in a shoebox.

Bush misses that money
so nearly every day he pins
the machine man up against the wall.
Dollar a day he loses
in those machines.

OLD GREEN

Old Green stops to say goodbye,
retiring after 43 years.
No green coveralls today.
Dressed in street clothes
hair slicked back
he even manages a shy smile
as I shake his hand.

The Company gave him an aerial photo
of the plant, and all the guys
sign their names around it
and *Good luck.*
All you can see is the roof
and the parking lots
and the tiny, tiny cars.
As hard as you look
you'll never find him.

SUGGESTION PROGRAM SUBMISSION FORM

Describe present method or condition.

Millrights & hi-lo with rack must be called to set feed on this press.

What specific improvement do you recommend?

Install ladder and stand adjacent to feed adjustment so die setter can safely adjust the feed.

What advantages can be expected from this change?

Safety of employees.

The foregoing idea is submitted under the Suggestion Program of my Employer with which I am familiar. In consideration of my participation in whichever Plan of the Program is applicable to me, the compensation paid to me as an employee and the facilities and data made available to me by my Employer (say what?) I hereby recognize as the exclusive property of, and assign, transfer and convey to my Employer any and all rights I may have to the whole or any part of this idea, including patent rights, if any, and I will execute any and all conveyances, assignments or other papers relating thereto which my Employer may request. I agree that any decision made by my Employer regarding eligibility, adoption, rejection, award or commendation with reference to my idea shall be final and binding, and that my Employer shall have the right to withdraw or change the Program at any time.

■

SUGGESTION/PROPOSAL DISPOSITION REPORT
REASON FOR NON-APPROVAL:

Installation of a permanent ladder and platform would hamper operations in the department and would have to be removed to perform repairs.

This case will be retained in our files for thirteen months from this date giving you rejection protection on it for that time. If you are still eligible, you can resubmit the idea any time during the thirteen months. *SHOULD YOU FAIL TO RESUBMIT AND THE IDEA IS LATER USED BY THE COMPANY OR LATER SUBMITTED BY SOMEONE ELSE, NO CONSIDERATION FOR AN AWARD OR COMMENDATION CAN BE GIVEN TO YOU FOR THIS CASE.*

WORK SONG: JUNIOR EDWARDS' STORY

Junior was a big dude—
rode with the Liberty Riders.
He had a few ugly scars
showed he was a fighter.

So he wasn't no fragile thing
but when the hot days came
he'd fall down in a crazy faint
rolled his eyes, played his game.

They'd carry him off.
A week later he'd come back sunburned
with a big laugh—
Santino tried to look stern.

Lookin' stern didn't faze
Junior—fists were his way.
He'd meet the foreman's gaze
till the foreman turned away.

Sick is sick, he'd wink at us
ain't nothing wrong about that.
We'd sit and glumly nod our heads
while he rubbed his fat.

One day it hit 110 degrees—
figured Junior'd take his dive
but Old Jess was the one
and it wasn't no jive.

I thought Junior'd start a fight
but he just threw his gloves down
(his face was pretty white)
and walked out that August day:
Jess is dead. And he was right.

I'd like to say we followed him
out into the sun
but we have no scars to our names
just wives, daughters, sons.

DISHING IT OUT

Gracie crunches toward the factory gate
over loose gravel, chewing a few
choice words to spit at anyone
gets in her way.

New security guard asks her
to open her lunch box.
She grunts, keeps on walking.
He grabs her arm, she turns
belts him with her pail, catches
his nose with a sharp edge.

He falls down, nose squirting blood.
She hurries into the tiny women's locker room
whiskey dripping from her broken flask.

Later, men will ask her questions
and send her home. When she steps out
into the plant now with Jeannie and Nita
we surround her. She slaps us high fives
and we feel the sting.

MIDNIGHT RAMBLE

This is the middle class, lower. The tree in the yard. Bushes in front of the house. Flowers in the yard. Lawn mowers growling. Dogs barking. Lots of dogs. Everybody has one, for safety, and they keep them locked up in their yards where they bark and bark behind their fences because no one ever takes them for a walk. Ice cream men. Lawn chairs. And beer and beer bellies and white paint on trim and brick and a hose at the side of the house. Squares, everything squares. Sidewalks and lawns and porches and houses and brains. TV sets. Garage sales and telephone poles. Kids sell kool-aid in summer, shovel snow in winter. Till they're old enough to smoke and drink and raise hell. They get a couple years of that, then it's factory time. Always one lawn mower going. Because everyone on this street works in a factory and they're all on different shifts. Maybe they communicate through their lawns, waking me here in the dark, damp basement. The young guys in the factory say they're not going to work there the rest of their lives. Just 'temporary.' The old guys laugh at that. They say *Temporary my ass.*

PHOTO OPPORTUNITY

I'm driving home from work late August
in my '68 Satellite down factory row
with Odie who's trying to grow
a mustache and trying this minute to light
a joint. He worked JAWS today,
the broacher that once ate a man's hands.
His hands are fine as he strikes
a match.

"Heaven on the Seventh Floor," a song
about being stuck in an elevator
with a beautiful woman, blasts
from my radio's only station
and I sing loud
for the first time in years, maybe
because Odie sings as bad as I do
or because I have a fat check in my pocket,
or because my job is like being stuck
in an elevator, so this song is alright by me.

Santino's on vacation, and his sub here
who looks like Dick Cavett
took us to Dept. 16 today,
the department of heavy lifting and misery.
I told him *Hell no.*
Odie's doing his Cavett imitation
but he's laughing so hard he can't say a word
so it seems like he's doing
his Crazy Wally imitation—Crazy Wally
who has never been on network television
works with us, constantly stoned and laughing
like that, and Odie, who has also never been
on television but does pretty good imitations
now mocks my anger at Cavett
making my *Hell no* sound
like a sonic boom.

We had to work in Dept. 16 anyway
throwing axle housings onto pallets
but when the line broke down
Cavett sent us home early,
early enough so when we get to my house
we take pictures of each other, happy
with a couple extra hours of energy
and light, and I'm standing
in the driveway holding a beer
headphones over my nose, laughing,
shouting *Hell no* when Odie pushes
the button down.

5 STEEL-TOED BOOT

PASS

Employee No. 6704

Leaving Plant 6:40

Reason: Breakdown

R. Santino

SOO LOCKS

for my mother

You talk about the Soo Locks
and how you love to watch the water
go up and down, and the boats,
and I laugh, *The water goes up
and down, big deal,*
and grab the lunch you made me
and run out the door
and drive to the job
to stack steel
and I watch the press go up and down
and the more it goes up and down
the more steel I have to stack.
I understand this up and down of the factory,
it is simple and American, machines and steel,
and I eat the lunch you made me
and close my eyes
and try to picture
the water going up and down.

BUT

Whenever I see a truck jacked up high so you can see the rear axle, I wonder if it's one of the ones I helped make. And when I pass the sign on the freeway keeping track of the number of new cars built in America, I think about how I helped make some of those cars.

But we don't have any control over how fast the number turns. But anyone can come in and press my two buttons. But I spend half my time trying to get away with *not* working. It seems like that's the only way to make a dent—to goof things up.

But if I goof things up and everyone else goofs things up then we'll all lose our jobs. But I'm paid well to push my two buttons.

But I don't have any say, finally. Maybe they're paying us just enough to keep us comfortable, just enough so we can go in debt for our houses and cars. Just enough to keep us numb and distracted and tired. Just enough. I watch the number slowly turn.

INDUSTRIAL INFECTION

These days my belly expands.
I loosen my belt and answer
to the name Chub.

Alice wants me to get
some respectable clothes.

I want to fuck the woman next door
the one with the long black hair.

THE FOREMAN'S BOOTH

Santino motions to me
with his finger
not touching me, not touching
my machine. Together
we go in his booth.

It's almost quiet in there,
like a stall in the john,
barely room for both of us.
I feel like an intruder
though we can all watch him there
through the glass
sitting on his stool
with his perpetual sulk
like a toll booth attendant.

And he can watch us.
He yells at me for coming back
from break late two days in a row.
I can hardly breathe
the heavy air, his voice muffled
back off the plexiglass.

Next break
I sit down at our picnic table
in front of the booth.
He looks up over his glasses
then down again.
He's busy with paperwork—
parts, time sheets, reports—
collecting our silent tolls.

FACTORY RAT

Rat: a) Any of various long-tailed rodents resembling, but larger than, mice. b) A despicable, sneaky person, especially one who betrays or informs upon his associates.

I smell a rat.

Factory: A building or group of buildings in which goods are manufactured; a plant.

Plant: A seemingly trivial passage or line in a play or story that becomes important later.

Plant: The equipment, including machinery, tools, instruments, and fixtures, and the buildings containing them, necessary for any industrial or manufacturing operation; factory.

Machinery. tools. instruments. fixtures. buildings. *I smell a rat.*

Plant: A scheming trick; a swindle. *Now we're on to something.*

24 BASKETS

I fill each basket with 180
banjo housing halves
in straight even rows,
throw cracked ones
into the scrap basket.

I count everything. How many
bites for this sandwich
how many steps to the car
how many stop lights on the way home
how many seconds till they change.

How many beers last night?
I don't know. How many cracked ones
in the scrap basket?

WORK SONG: BLUES FOR ME, BLUES FOR JEANNIE

A beautiful woman works
down the line from me
dressed in baggy coveralls
but still you can see.

Closest I've been, she was
slamming brakes with me.
Closest I've been—
I would've worked for free.

Me on the left side
her on the right.
Tried to get her grinning
but she was tight.

I said *I'm not like*
She said *Heard that before*
I said *I swear I*
She said *Heard that before.*

Walking toward the lockers
she offered me a smoke.
I smiled when she lit it
She said *What's the joke?*

I guess I'm like the others
blowing smoke in her face.
I've seen Santino grab her—
he's always on her case.

But I love that woman, I tell Odie.
He says, *No room for love in here.*
It's not just her looks, I tell him.
He says *C'mon, let's grab a beer.*

And we punch out, wash the grease
off our hands, step out the gate
where the fresh air beats
beats against my face. Her face.

THE PLANT NURSE'S STORY

Some guy walked in
and said he needed a pass
to go home. I said
What's wrong with you?
He said
I just need a pass to go home.
I said
There has to be something wrong with you
or I can't send you home.
He said
I'm gonna kill my foreman.
I said
Calm down for a few minutes
and then go back to work.
He said
I'm gonna kill that motherfucker
then walked out
so I never knew
who his foreman was
till they brought him in
all smashed up.
He was a mess, I tell you.

I didn't think
he was serious.
I mean I hear
that kind of talk
all the time.

BUSH'S STORY

Been here 22 years
never had no trouble.
But when a foreman messes
in my shit I get hot—
especially some punk like Cavett.
That little prick never got dirty
never touched a machine.
Just pointed. Reminded me
of one of those pretty boys
does the tv news.

I didn't want to hurt him.
Just wanted to scare him—
back his ass against a wall, get him
a little greasy. Make him feel
the hot air blowing out the hi-lo.

You shoulda seen his face.
I just couldn't stop.

CHRISTMAS IN THE FACTORY

We get the week off between Christmas and New Year's.
The whole plant. Day before break, everyone's drunk.

Odie hands me a half-pint: *Cheers, Digger.*
Santino's loose, rocking on his heels,
sticking his belly out.

Santa wanders through the plant on a hi-lo.
I'm no true believer
but I stick around after work
slapping backs and poking ribs.

∎

Christmas Day I drive by on my way to Alice's.
Clean snow blows across the empty parking lot.
If not for the high fences
I could imagine a lake under there,
the pure, clear ice.

The snow plows will be here soon
with their lights and beepers
to scrape the yellow lines clear.

Inside, the clocks are still ticking.

STACKING

As soon as the front stack of blanks
dwindles down to about 10
I sit on the rollers and kick
in a new stack of 60
careful to keep it from tipping,
wedging it slow into the slot.
Sweat drips onto the metal blanks.

I cut myself on a blank—sharp edge—
common occurrence—but this one's deep.
I watch blood pour down my arm
and onto the blanks like I'm watching
a drinking fountain. Till Odie grabs me,
drags me to Santino's booth—
Give him a pass to the hospital, he shouts.
Santino looks, nods. I stand quietly
as he writes my name, ss#, and the time,
then walk through the plant
holding paper towels to my arm.
In the air-conditioned plant hospital
I sit down bleeding. The nurse looks at me
from the desk. Yells
Watch, you're dripping.
I get my arm stitched up
and go back to work
full of something soft, warm
as if my own blood spilling
let the hardness out.
I overstack to leave plenty
for the next shift, smiling to myself,
careful.

ELEPHANT HOUSE

The john smells like an elephant house.

I'm an elephant standing here emptying
my trunk, pressing my face into the tile.

Elephant jokes were popular once
as substitutes for ethnic jokes.
You couldn't get anyone in here
to listen to an elephant joke.

I can't go much further with this
I'm afraid. I am not an elephant.

∎

I make a headband from paper towels.
I'm an Indian. Splashing water on my face
from the bathroom stream. I'm on a journey.
I'm lost. The face in the mirror
is my enemy. I splash the water
and splash the water. I try to breathe.
I am not an Indian.

AFTER WORK

A heavy snow sparkles under the streetlight
as I pull in front of the house.
It was another day of welding axle housings.
I punched in. I welded. I punched out.
I pressed the idiot buttons
watched the machine weld
a circle around the pale steel.
Damned hard to hurt yourself
with both hands on those buttons
Santino told me my first day.
On the way home, I skidded into a ditch.
Cost me twenty for the tow.

I don't want to go in
to this dark, quiet house
to see my family sleeping
clean, safe, warm
don't want to see my dog
curled on the floor
kicking his legs through dreams.

Tonight I open the gate
and toss my lunch bucket
in a drift by the door.
I fall face down and twist
my head until I hit cement.
I pound idiot buttons into the snow.
Maybe this is what I want,
the cold stars pressing
against my face.

ODIE'S LAST DAY

He moves slow today, not caring about foremen
or general foremen or superintendents.
The boys on the line come up:
This your last day? You quitting?
He nods. They wink.

Here our hearts get buried under grease,
labeled defective, thrown out as scrap.
Bush told me once *Friendly*
don't count for shit in here.
But I think finally he was wrong.

All night Odie's machine breaks.
No one can seem to fix it. He sits down.
Wally gives him some herb superb
to smoke at lunch.
We watch the clock tick
and wait, telling him our stories,
the ones we all have memorized
about when we quit.

PIECES

I used to think Wally Chimes got by
on religion, lugging that Bible around
quoting, big smile on his face.
Till I found him blowing a joint
out by the factory gate.
I said *Wally, what's with this?*
Where's Jesus? He said *Jesus*
ain't enough for this place, bro
and handed me the joint.

∎

Spooner in his big silk hat
drips ashes onto the racing form.
He's hurried over from the track
to make midnight shift. *Got to earn*
the money I lost today. He taps
the form against his head
to the rhythm of the presses.

∎

Santino fills out suggestions
for the company program. We fill in our names
and get a flashlight. With 100% employee participation
he gets a clock radio. In *Ford World*
we read about a guy who gets a car.
Think big, Santino. Get that car, we tell him.
He's looking around, taking notes.

∎

Odie read books on break
talked about graduating from college,
saving money, getting married,
buying a house, starting a family.
Becoming management. *Like Santino?*
He lit a cigarette off a hot weld,
squinted at me till I turned away.

■

Andy in Heat Treat is the Drugstore.
Wally Chimes sent me, I say.
He shows his teeth: *That asshole.*
Pot? Is that all you want? Listen
dude, you're on midnights—
how about speed?

After he knows me
he likes to punch me hard
now and then, like that's part
of my payment for being smart enough
to skip his habit.
I never punch him back.

■

At the end of the shift
I sit at the break table
staring into darkness and grease
thinking it doesn't matter
if I stay or go home.

Santino stands, hands on hips: *What*
the hell you sittin' around for?
Go home and get yourself
a piece of ass. I turn to him,
I am a piece of ass.
He laughs at that
so I say it louder.